Clarify Your Purpose
and
LIVE IT

Live your purpose
with passion!

5. 24. 2011

Clarify Your Purpose
and
LIVE IT

THE THOUGHT DR.™
PATRICIA OMOQUI
WITH GAYLE DULCEY

Clarify Your Purpose
and
LIVE IT

Printed in the United States of America.
ISBN 13: 978-0-9829129-0-4 • ISBN 10: 0-9829129-0-0
LCCN: 2010911347
SEL027000 SELF-HELP / Personal Growth / Success
First Edition
1 2 3 4 5 6 7 8 9 10

BOOKS
www.bluetailbooks.com

Patricia Omoqui Enterprises
PO Box 1547 • Lansdale, PA 19446
patricia@patriciaomoqui.com

Visit us on the web!
www.patriciaomoqui.com

Dedication

I dedicate this book to the legacy of love and integrity of my
father-in-law and mother-in-law,

Felix Idemudia Omoqui

(1924 – 2010)

and

Margaret Adafor Omoqui,

(1931 – 2001).

My husband David and I feel their spirits guiding and
supporting us as we move forward in our life journey.

Table of Contents

Acknowledgements

A number of talented and generous people tirelessly assisted me behind the scenes to bring this book to completion.

To Joanie Littrel, Elizabeth Onyeabor, Carol Coale, Miriam Dynan, Maple Dappa and Paul Geissler, please accept my sincere gratitude for your hard work in reading the text, doing the exercises, sharing your insights and proofreading.

To Carrie Draghi, my dear friend and soul sister, I am delighted with the brilliant photography you provided for the book cover. You are incredibly talented and generous.

To my husband David and my daughters, Maggie and Skye, thank you for encouraging me and cheering me on during this long and intense process.

To my mom, Gayle Dulcey, words cannot express my appreciation for the endless hours of discussion and editing you put into the creation of this book. Your wisdom deepened each chapter and helped me order and fine-tune every concept. You are the most patient, giving and loving woman I know. I would not have been able to complete this book without your always-present support—all provided on an unbelievably compressed production schedule.

Introduction

Wake Up to Your Life and Purpose

KEY QUESTIONS:
Why am I here? What is my purpose?

AFFIRMATIONS:
I wake up to my life. I wake up to my power.

Take a moment to reflect on your life. Why are you here? Where are you headed? Is your job unsatisfying? Are your relationships stressful? Are finances burdensome? Are you plagued by an underlying sense of psychological and physical malaise? Have your youthful dreams for a happy, successful life faded?

If you answered, "Yes," to any or all of these questions, you are probably functioning in survival mode, enduring life rather than relishing it. This need not be. *If you want to move in a positive direction and you are willing to learn, there is hope!*

Your inner voice has no doubt whispered to you, "There is something more to all of this. I am made to be happy. Surely, my life has a purpose."

God did not create you to tolerate life as endless drudgery. We are eternal spirits in physical bodies here to live in meaningful, satisfying ways. You can learn to move through your days confident that you are on earth for an important reason. I encourage you to open your heart to this possibility.

For the last three years, I have been writing a weekly feature column for Vanguard Newspaper's Sunday magazine, *Allure* (Nigeria). Every day, I respond to emails from readers. These interactions often inspire new articles. One topic that repeatedly comes up is how to find your life purpose and live it. Readers are hungry to explore this topic.

The chapters in this book emerged from articles I wrote to address the question of one's life purpose from various angles. I have expanded and deepened the material and made it into a basic roadmap to self-discovery. If you follow this "map," it will help you to know yourself and expand your vision of what is possible for you.

Clarify Your Purpose and Live It was not designed to be a quick read. All the chapters are connected and presented in an order that flows. Each chapter invites you to closely examine an important issue or challenge that people often face as they pursue a purpose-rich life. Chapters open with a key question and affirmation. Next follows the discussion of an important concept. Each chapter ends with a practical exercise and inspiring quotations.

In order to get the most out of this book, I encourage you to *do the exercises.* Dedicate a notebook or journal to this process of clarifying your life purpose. Do not underestimate the value of writing out your responses to the exercises. When you record your answers, you will find that you capture surprising reactions, valuable "aha's," and other significant personal insights— crucial details that may otherwise slip away. Transformation is the natural outgrowth of the increased awareness that comes from a determined positive mental focus.

Living with purpose is a life-long commitment. This book can help you to make a start or take you to the next level of understanding your purpose. I trust you will be guided to use it in the way that is best for you.

Have fun. Savor the process. The joy is not in the destination as much as it is in each moment of the journey. Enjoy every step on this journey to *Clarify Your Purpose and Live It!*

Thank you for allowing me to be a part of it.

With Warm Regards,
Patricia

Chapter One

Leave a Legacy
of Love

KEY QUESTION:

How do I want to be remembered when my journey is done?

AFFIRMATION:

I open to my deeper purpose.

It was March 24, 2010. My heart was full. I sat with my five-year-old daughter, Skye, in front of me gently undoing the braids in her hair. As I worked I experienced both grief and celebration.

One month before, my husband, David, had traveled to Nigeria to visit his 86-year-old father, Felix Idemudia Omoqui. At the time, David and I lived in the United States. We had received reports that Papa's health was failing. David wanted to see his dad one last time. He flew to Lagos with plans to proceed immediately to Benin for this treasured visit. Then he received a call from his sister. David's last visit with his father was not to be. Papa had just passed away.

The news stunned us all. Papa Omoqui was one of the strongest men I have known. He walked in honesty and faith, expressing kindness to all who knew him.

I met Papa Omoqui in January 2000. It was my first visit to Nigeria. David and I were engaged to be married. I knew his parents wondered what kind of "Oyinbo" David was bringing to their home. Of course, I was nervous about meeting my future in-laws. How would they receive me?

When I arrived at Lagos International Airport, Mr. and Mrs. Omoqui greeted me with open arms and open hearts. During my stay, they showered me with hospitality and love. I was welcomed into the family without hesitation.

In August 2001, Papa and Mama Omoqui visited the United States to participate in our marriage ceremony. I had the honor of spending almost two months with them. They were delightful, encouraging and eager to experience American culture.

A few weeks after their return to Nigeria, Maragaret Adafor Omoqui died suddenly as a result of a heart condition. It was a devastating blow to our family. Just one month earlier, I had helped Mama pack suitcases full of goodies to take home to her family, friends and neighbors. The bags bulged so much that I feared the zippers would split before the bags reached their destination.

A year later we named our first daughter "Margaret" to honor her grandmother's legacy of love.

Now it was 2010. Again, grief touched our family when Papa Omoqui passed away. His death awakened me to a deeper contemplation of life. Why am I here? What is my purpose?

Felix Omoqui did not focus on amassing properties, titles or millions of Naira. Though he was recognized among his peers for his intelligence. He refused to participate in the bribery and stealing so prevalent in the workplace. He was such a principled man that he often walked away from jobs because he would not compromise his moral standards. When Papa Omoqui died, he left a legacy of love and integrity that will be carried on in the hearts and lives of his children and grandchildren.

On March 15, 2010, I received word of another shocking loss.

Removing the braids from my youngest daughter, Skye's, hair should be an ordinary experience. It was not this time. These braids were special. These braids were made by a 16-year-old Sierra Leonian girl named Mattu. "Why is that a big deal?" you might ask. Let me explain.

Several months earlier, I met Mattu at a local restaurant through a mutual friend. She noticed that my girls' hair needed braiding and kindly offered her services. We accepted and opened the door to a friendship that grew quickly into shared meals and enjoyable times with Mattu and her brothers and sisters.

Mattu became dear to us. We were saddened when she told us she was moving to Florida with her family. On her last evening in our neighborhood, she joined us for dinner and braided Skye's hair one last time. On Saturday, March 13, we bid Mattu and her family goodbye, comforted by the promise of her return to Philadelphia for a summer visit.

The following Monday I received a phone call, "Mattu is gone! She was hit by a car and killed instantly." I tried to comprehend the words. My whole body went numb. "What? Are you sure? This can't be true!" The reply was simple and somber, "I'm sorry."

Two weeks later I attended Mattu's memorial service given by friends in the Philadelphia area. I was struck deeply by the words of many who shared their memories with the group. Mattu had touched each of them with her joyfully vibrant spirit. She is remembered as a happy young woman who loved friends and food and shared everything she had with her mother and siblings.

Now, as I was unraveling the braids that Mattu had woven in Skye's hair, I was smiling through tears remembering Mattu and her laughter, still touched by her generosity.

As I moved through the days during the spring of 2010, I often experienced surges of grief followed by waves of joy. These deaths made me poignantly aware of the fragility and mystery of life. A beloved father joined his wife in heaven after 86 full years; a beautiful young woman was called home by God at age 16. Both are remembered for the greatest legacy anyone can leave: L-O-V-E.

What is your purpose? What legacy will you leave? What do you want to be remembered for? Do not rush through these questions. Contemplate them. Meditate on them. Open your heart. Why not make a conscious decision about the way you will choose to live each day?

Life does not come down to who has the biggest house or the most expensive jewelry. It has little to do with the highest title or the fattest bank account. Rather, life comes down to simple acts of warmth and acceptance. Each kind gesture is a deposit we make in the hearts of those we meet. A smile, an uplifting word, a prayer said on someone's behalf, a meal prepared with care, time spent listening, laughing and sharing in meaningful conversation—any act of compassion or understanding makes a lasting impression.

Here are a few key questions to ponder as you begin to clarify your purpose in life.

1. Are you sleepwalking, allowing days to slip by, feeling depressed, disheartened and unsure of where you are headed? If life feels dreary and gray to you, if you find yourself wandering aimlessly about, open to the exquisite realities of life all around you. Come alive to the moment. Ordinary moments are extraordinary when you engage your senses fully. Wake up to your life!

2. What will they say about you? How do you want to be remembered? Take time to formulate one or two statements that express what you want people to say about you. I'll share mine. I want people to say, "She accepted me where I was and helped me to see and reach my full potential."

3. Once you have clarified the way you desire to be remembered, ask yourself, "How could my interests, gifts and assets be used in a way that will fulfill my desire?" Then begin to take daily action. Use your passions, talents and resources in any way you can right now.

4. Are you obsessing over debilitating details—what someone else thinks about you, what someone has said about you or ways you feel deprived? If so, conserve your energy. Lighten up about life. Remember that much of what we worry about is frivolous and 99.9 percent of our fears never materialize. Einstein said, "I want to know God's thoughts; the rest are details." Ask to know God's thoughts. Keep your mind tuned in to the grand Mind that dissolves all problems and leads to wholeness.

5. How can you fill ordinary moments with love? Do not underestimate the importance of offering a kind word or a listening ear, sharing a meal with someone who is hungry or giving the extra money in your pocket to someone in need. Adopt the philosophy of Mother Teresa, "What I do you cannot do; but what you do, I cannot do. The needs are great, and none of us, including me, ever do great things. But we can all do small things, with great love, and together we can do something wonderful."

None of us knows how long we will be here. Commit to clarifying your purpose. And in the meantime, let's bring every moment alive by filling it with all the love we can muster. If you use these questions as a daily guide, you will place yourself in the perfect situations and frame of mind to further clarify your life purpose.

Thank you for joining me on this journey. Let's get started.

EXERCISE:

Isn't it interesting that after all the peaks and valleys, our life journey is summed up by one simple dash? Let me explain. When we attend a funeral, we usually receive a memorial card or program. Almost always, the person's name appears at the top and beneath it their birth year, a dash and their final year (for example, 1939 – 2009). This little dash represents the person's whole life.

At a funeral people honor the person's "Dash": what they stood for, what they accomplished and most important, who they were.

What do you want your "Dash" to mean? Get clear now. Remember, no matter how many arrows you shoot, you will never hit a target unless you are aiming at it. Use the following steps to get a high-level view of your life's aim.

Take a few minutes to sit quietly. Contemplate what you want people to say about you when your earthly journey has ended.

When you are ready, get your journal and move through the following steps:

1. Excavate. When people are at my funeral describing my "Dash," what do I want them to remember me for? Keep in mind the character traits you want your loved ones to mention. Consider the accomplishments you'd like people to recall. Reflect on the way you want to touch the lives of those around you.

Open the door to your heart and let your creative juices flow. This is your opportunity to discover your deeper purpose. Do not worry about HOW it can happen. Just answer the questions honestly.

2. Summarize. When you are finished writing, try to reduce the way you want to be remembered to one short paragraph. Do your best. Do not worry about "getting this right."

3. Pinpoint. Focus precisely on the way you want to be remembered. Try to write an epitaph for your gravestone. It could be as simple as "She brought joy," "He cared," "She was a faithful wife, mother and friend," or "He shared his wealth with others."

Whatever comes from your heart is right for you in this moment. Your statement of purpose is a work in progress. You can add to it, refresh it or change it as often as you'd like. In fact, it would be wise to revisit this statement on each birthday or New Year's Day to keep it fresh in your heart and mind.

Meditation: Food For Thought

"The question is not whether we will die, but how we will live."
—Joan Borysenko

"When you were born, you cried and the world rejoiced. Live your life so that when you die, the world cries and you rejoice."
—Wisdom from the Cherokee Indians

Chapter Two

Get to
Know Yourself

KEY QUESTION:
How do I REALLY feel about my life?

AFFIRMATION:
I tune in to the way I feel about my life and stay tuned in.

I have been getting to know myself better over the last several years, years of significant change. Each change, large and small, was sparked by a moment when I gained an insight about myself and worked with it. I began transforming my life from the inside out when I started monitoring my inner systems candidly. The power I gained from these transformations has increased my desire to know myself and be true to myself.

Learning to Look Within

We underestimate the importance of growing our awareness of ourselves. We pretend that everything is okay and we suppress our inner discomfort. We stoically give the impression that, "Everything is just fine," even if we are torn with conflict, seething with rage or weighed down by depression.

Through my twenties I anesthetized my inner self. I focused on outward circumstances and achievements that others told me represented a successful life.

I suppressed the occasional, deep longing for something more that rose from within. I found plenty of ways to numb myself, from workouts at the gym, to nights out with friends, to focusing upon my professional goals.

Rather than tuning into my persistent inner broadcast that repeated: "I don't like my life!" I lived in a state of endless "noise" comprised of continual thinking, never-ending activity and relentless attempts to find comfort in possessions or relationships. I resisted seeing or knowing myself. I tried to drown out my voice of truth.

Though I persistently ignored my voice of truth, life faithfully offered me emotional, physical and relational signals, "You need a change."

I was often on the verge of tears while dealing with life's challenges. I was physically exhausted and even experienced sharp pains in my chest. Conflict colored many of my closest relationships.

Despite these calls to wake up, I focused on finding the next "fix" to maintain my status quo. Even as I saw myself approaching a breakdown, I seriously considered adding an additional 20 to 40 hours of graduate classes to my absurdly busy weekly schedule. I believed I would feel better if I obtained a Master's in Business Administration.

In retrospect, there were many clues—my whole being was begging for change. I was deaf and blind to the built-in warning systems that were sending a clear message: "I AM UNHAPPY."

Something needed to give. Finally my suffering became so intense that I was forced to turn my attention to what was happening in my life.

At first, self-honesty was followed by self-judgment. I felt the pain of guilt and shame. "How could I have gotten myself into this situation? I should have known better. I was so foolish to take this job, choose this apartment and initiate these friendships."

Gradually, I made peace with the past. There was nothing I could do to change it. However, I could learn from my experiences as I moved forward. The self-recrimination subsided.

Taking a Deeper Look

I began to consciously review my life. What felt bad to me? What didn't I like? I also took stock of the good things. What made me content? What made me feel well? What did I really enjoy?

I had tolerated mild and intense suffering because somewhere along the line I had bought into the belief that "suffering is a natural part of life." I thought I must "grin and bear" things, no matter what. Now I opened to a different perspective. Could there be a way to enjoy every day and even walk through times of intensity free of suffering? Did I have more power to change my circumstances than I realized?

I decided to explore the possibilities.

Ignoring the Indications

I discovered that we are created with built-in systems that tell us whether we are in or out of alignment with ourselves. I could no longer ignore the signals. It was my responsibility to stop, look and listen. It is up to us to get honest with ourselves.

Are you ready to tune into yourself? If so, you can follow your own inner guidance toward a happy, healthy, joyful life. These systems work if you are willing to pay attention to them.

If you will join me in taking a look at these inner systems, you will find your own best way to start the process of knowing yourself better.

Pay Attention to Your Emotions

Your emotions offer moment-to-moment feedback. They are like an emotional compass. Your emotions tell you what does and does not work in your life. You can become an expert on yourself by fully acknowledging and consciously experiencing each emotion as it arises.

Begin by noticing positive emotions. Pleasant emotions like peace, hope and gratitude tell us we are on the right track. Now begin to monitor your negative emotions. Do you regularly feel sadness, anger, jealousy, depression, hurt or fear? If so, be thankful. Just like your positive emotions, these unpleasant ones are a gift from the Divine. Negative emotions are like inner sirens. They say, "You have an issue here. . . . This is a growth point, do not ignore it. . . . Dealing with this will lead you to greater personal freedom. . . ."

Rather than avoiding or denying your emotions, begin to feel each of them fully. Ask for insight about the causes fueling each one. What is causing this fear? Why do you feel hope? What just made you smile? Why are you jealous?

Notice that your emotions and beliefs are intertwined. We are integrated beings. From the time we are children, we get a response when we say or do something. The response generates a positive or negative emotion. Our minds then draw a conclusion and form a belief. For example, you tell the truth and you are rebuked. Feeling embarrassed by this response you form a belief: "If I tell the truth I'm going to be humiliated. I had better be very careful about what I say." Until you call this belief into question, it will remain in operation. Once you understand what underlies your emotions, you will know how to consciously move beyond limiting beliefs toward beliefs and experiences that help you feel good.

Observe Your Thoughts

For some people honesty begins by working with their emotions. Others find it easier to begin by observing their thoughts. Your thoughts reflect your beliefs about life. Some are limiting you; others lead you to freedom. Do not accept your thoughts without question. Become a detective and look for clues. Notice the emotional response that follows a thought you are focusing on.

Also, pay particular attention to the thought sequences that play repeatedly in your mind. For example, consider this train of thought/emotion: "I didn't finish all the documents I was asked to do today. . . . (Emotion: disappointment). . . . I am not competent. . . . (Emotion: shame). . . . I'll never get a promotion . . . . (Emotion: fear). . . . In fact, I do not even deserve this job. . . . (Emotion: self-anger). . . . Everybody else is better than I am. . . . (Emotion: self-pity). . . . What's the use in trying? . . . . (Emotion: resignation, depression)." Become alert to negative self-talk and debilitating emotions that accompany it. These patterns keep you chained to old ways.

Listen to Your Body

Listening to your body is another way to become honest with yourself. Your body is continually processing your thoughts and emotions. Take a few moments to sit still or lie down. Slowly scan your body from head to toe. Are you relaxed or do you feel stressed? Do any areas feel really good? Appreciate them. Are there tense spots? What is causing this tension? Do you need more rest? Do you have a physical malady that needs attention? Are you being abused in some way? Is your body suffering from the results of addiction to drugs, alcohol, food or sex?

Focus your energy on a stressed area in your body. Ask your body what it needs. Then pause and listen to what it says. Your body never lies. Hold the stressed area in your attention and wait for insight.

What did you discover? Listening to your body is an important step in self-discovery. If your issues are complex, you may need to seek the assistance of qualified doctors, mental health professionals, pastors or addiction counselors. When you are ready for change, you will be guided to the next steps.

Capitalize on Your Intuition

Gut reactions and inner knowing are intuitions. Intuition is the ability to know directly without having concrete information. Have you ever felt a bad vibe when you met someone? Perhaps you sensed that something was amiss or that you should keep your distance. When this happens, you are reading another person's energy. Intuition is a gift from your Creator. You are receiving guidance to help you make your journey easier. Do not ignore or suppress this inner knowing. Honor it.

Use Discomfort as Guidance

Now that you are aware of inner guidance systems, use them to take a look at your life. What in your life feels restrictive? Let your conflicts surface. Are you miserable in your job? Do you dread going home at night? Admit these things to yourself instead of suppressing them. Personal discomfort is valuable information. Do not avoid it. Feel it. Understand it. Explore it.

Inner or outer uneasiness indicates an opportunity for learning and growth.

Do not assume that misery is a necessary part of life. As a friend of mine says, "Suffering is overrated." We have more power to change the way we live than we generally acknowledge.

Self-honesty is the place to begin reclaiming that power.

EXERCISE:

Take a look at each of your inner systems and the insights they are offering. Be as honest as possible when you answer these questions.

1. What emotions have you been feeling lately? Take time to list the positive and negative emotions. Then ask yourself, "Why am I feeling this way?" Write your answers down.

2. What thoughts are causing you guilt, worry, insecurity or depression? Write down each stressful thought. Seeing them in black and white will make you clearer about the way your mind is operating.

3. How does your body feel? What signals is it giving you? Note any areas of discomfort or pain. What steps can you take to feel better?

4. What intuitions have you received recently? What inner knowing have you acted upon? Which ones are you dismissing?

5. Are there areas of life that are causing you discomfort? Name the person, place or situation. What steps can you take to reduce or eliminate this uneasiness?

6. Post the following question in a place you will see it every day: "What are my emotions, thoughts, body, intuition and life discomforts showing me about myself?"

Meditation: Food For Thought

"Extreme hopes are born out of extreme misery."
—Bertrand Russell

"Deep, unspeakable suffering may well be called a baptism,
a regeneration, the initiation into a new state."
—George Eliot

"No one can give you better advice than yourself."
—Cicero

Chapter Three

Turn Negatives into Positives

KEY QUESTION:
How can I shift my focus from what I do not like to what I do like?

AFFIRMATION:
I turn negative experiences into helpful insights.

Most clients who seek me out as a life coach want to feel better. They are eager for change. Yet when I ask them exactly what type of change they want to make, they cannot name specifics. They do not know what they want.

Negatives Are a Place to Begin – When You Are Ready

There is something that all of us do know. We can all describe what we DO NOT want to experience. In fact, most people I meet are experts at complaining in detail about conditions at work or home, chores they dislike and people who annoy them.

If your continual focus is on what you do not want, you will continue to generate more of what you do not want. On the other hand, if you are not clear on what you DO want, try this: use your complaints as expertise. Examine what you dislike. Each thing you feel negative about is a clue to follow on your path to discovering what you really do desire.

Choose one area where you long for change: a relationship, your finances, your health, your career, your personal life or your spirituality and begin there. That is how I started. Learning what you consider as essential to a happy life takes time, energy and focus.

It is usually a process that occurs gradually. Rather than becoming overwhelmed by trying to clarify my vision or every aspect of life at once, I took a step back.

I was unhappy and confused. I often told my husband how much I disliked my job. He repeatedly asked, "Trish, what do you want to do?" The answer I became famous for was, "I don't know." I see now that I was actually saying, "Please let me alone! I am not ready to answer this question." Fortunately, David was persistent. His question eventually broke through my resistance and stimulated my thinking. What was I really looking for?

Write Your List: Turn Negatives into Positives

At last I was ready for change. I chose my career as my first focal point. I used my complaints. I began to list the things I did not want to experience in my next career.

For instance, I knew that I did not want to be confined to an office for eight hours a day. So what did I want? Answering this question produced increasing clarity. I wanted a career in which I could move around, lead teams and perhaps, work from many locations.

Furthermore, I did not want to be assigned major projects that I found boring. I wanted to continue managing projects and people. I wanted a challenge, an interesting assignment that would expose me to new content and allow me to develop additional skills. I wanted to be among dynamic people. In fact, I wanted to be dynamic myself, passionate about my work. I wanted to interact with others not just as workers completing tasks efficiently and effectively for "The Company," but as people growing personally. Ultimately, I realized I wanted to focus on helping others realize their full potential.

This initial list provided a starting point. The process of self-discovery unfolded over the following months as I gained increasing clarity. I listed my ideas in a journal so I could track my findings. I would work on my list and then spend time in reflection. I listened to my inner voice. Often, at the most unexpected times, suggestions came—from people, books and even billboards. As I maintained a steady focus and an attitude of openness to Divine guidance, I had more and more "aha" moments.

Breakthroughs Do Come

By beginning with what I did not want to be, experience and feel, I was able to define the things I did want to be, experience and feel. Through the months of contemplation I continued to use my journal. My inner exploration gradually broadened to touch my relationships, marriage, finances, physical health and personal dreams. My approach became holistic. I realized I did not want a career that dictated my lifestyle. My question then became, "What career could I pursue that would integrate with the lifestyle I am seeking?"

Before I knew it I had a good sense of the direction I wanted to move. I wanted a lifestyle where my family came first. I wanted harmonious relationships. I wanted to support myself financially by helping others reach their full potential. I wanted to travel frequently.

I had listed all the elements that would make me feel good in my new career. I also gained a growing understanding of the lifestyle that would accompany it.

I had made a beginning. I had used my negatives to develop criteria for what I wanted in life.

EXERCISE:

Now it is your turn. List the areas in your life in which you long for change.

1. Which area seems most pressing to you? Circle it. That's the place to begin.

2. Make two columns on a piece of paper. Label the first column "What I DO NOT like / want" and label the second column, "What I DO like / want."

My Career

What I DO NOT Like/Want	What I DO Like/Want
Example: *I don't want to be confined to a desk all day.*	*I want to be on the move.* *I want to work in a variety of locations.*

3. Start with the first column. List all of the items you know you DO NOT want.

4. Look at each item you listed in the first column. Transform it into a statement describing what you would like to experience.

5. Write down any additional insights that come to mind about what you truly desire. Continue growing your What I DO Like/Want list.

6. As you are ready, start a list for other major areas of your life. Remember, all aspects are interconnected. Consider these categories: Marriage, Friendship, Spirituality, Money/Finances, Health, Personal Growth, Career, Personal Ambition or make your own.

Meditation: Food For Thought

"In our consciousness, there are many negative seeds and also
many positive seeds. The practice is to avoid watering the
negative seeds, and to identify and water the positive seeds
every day."
—Thich Nhat Hanh

"Adopting the right attitude can convert a negative stress into
a positive one."
—Hans Selye

"Dwelling on the negative simply contributes to its power."
—Shirley MacLaine

Chapter Four

Celebrate What Is

KEY QUESTION:
What good is in my life already?

AFFIRMATION:
I am grateful for the good in my current circumstances.
There are blessings in every moment.

Although I had determined what I did not like about my life and was growing a list of what I did want, my outer circumstances had not changed. I was still functioning in the same job, carrying out the same responsibilities, living in the same apartment and facing the same daily challenges.

I could see that my old habits of dissatisfaction, inner complaining and dislike for my daily life drained my energy. I felt frustrated that I did not already have all the things I now knew I wanted. However, I had to be practical. Changing my circumstances would take some time. I needed to practice patience.

I remembered a quote I found in my high school years, "Happiness is not having what you want, it is wanting what you have." I used it in college as a way of cultivating gratitude. I would use it again.

I began to look actively for all the good in my life. I found it to be an essential step in moving forward to significant, positive change. Cultivating gratitude renewed my energy and cleared my mind. It lifted my spirit so that I could dream and create an even clearer vision for my next chapter.

During this period, a line from India Arie's song, "There's Hope," captured my attention: "It doesn't cost a thing to smile;

you don't have to pay to laugh—you better thank God for that."
Free resources. I found myself remembering more of the free
inner and outer resources God offers. They are available to rich
and poor, people of all ages, people of all walks of life and people
of all states of health. These generous resources belong to you.
They are waiting for you to notice and enjoy them. These gifts
are ours simply because we are alive.

In moments of deep contemplation I became more acutely
aware of these free resources and blessings. The ones I've listed
below are just a small sampling. As you read, perhaps you will
think of some of your own.

Free Inner Resources

We have the breath of life. Most of us breathe on auto-pilot.
When stress kicks in, our breath tends to become quick and
shallow. However, we can learn to breathe deeply and con-
sciously. Your breath can put you in touch with the life force
within you. It can make you aware of the inner aliveness that
permeates your whole body. Use your breath to cleanse your
body and mind. Breathe in refreshment; breathe out stress.
When you watch your breath, you naturally pull your attention
back to the present moment.

We are equipped with humor and laughter. Cracking a joke costs nothing. Telling or listening to a funny parable can lead to some hearty belly laughs and connect you in warm ways with others. Studies have shown that laughter boosts the immune system, decreases stress hormones and lowers blood pressure. Why not call someone who gets you laughing or learn a new joke to share with your co-workers? Those who say, "Laughter is the best medicine," are telling the truth.

We are designed to express love and kindness. How many smiles do you have that you can share with others? An endless supply! And offering one usually brings one or more in return. Moving through the day with a smile is likely to improve it in amazing ways. Helping someone with a heavy package, giving someone your seat on the bus and patting someone on the back for a job well done are all no-cost ways to express kindness and increase your own well-being.

Studies have shown that there are physical and emotional health benefits to being kind. Stress-related health problems, like depression, often improve in those performing acts of kindness. The sense of well-being that comes from doing good deeds can last for hours or even days. Thoughtfulness improves our feelings of self-worth, happiness and hopefulness.

Our bodies are made to move. You have a body pulsing with life energy. Why not focus more of that vigor in ways that help you feel well? Simply using your body to walk can energize you and elevate your mood. Instead of taking a motorbike, bus or taxi from one point to another why not walk part of the way?

Stretch. Stand on your tip toes. Flex your fingers. Roll your shoulders. Release the tension. Reach your hands to touch the sky. Tap your foot to some good music. Get off your seat and dance! No matter what physical challenges you may be experiencing, your inner self will guide you to movements that work for you.

Our minds are made to imagine and create. It doesn't cost a cent to daydream and play with ideas. You can start by traveling in your mind to beautiful places you see in magazine or TV advertisements. You may be surprised to find that these mental jaunts later turn into actual physical journeys.

Make use of your connection to the Divine. God does not charge a per-prayer fee. God also does not charge a per-load cost for the burdens you hand over! Inner hope is free of charge. Moments of quiet contemplation are yours to access as often as you choose. Why not enjoy the comfort of these rich resources?

Outer Resources

Nature's beauty beckons you. Have you noticed the palm trees lately? When is the last time you really felt a gentle breeze against your skin? Masterpieces of nature—sunrises, sunsets, stars and clouds—surround us. Take time to appreciate these fantastic displays of creativity.

Let nature inspire you. Humans invented airplanes after observing the amazing flight of birds. See all of nature's symbols. Could a tree remind you of how tall you are able to stand or how important it is to have deep roots? Will a bird help you see the possibility of flying higher in your life? The answer is up to you.

Children remind us of innocence and joy. Observing little ones is a wonderful way to remember your innate ability to play. Listening to their banter can give you a chuckle and lighten your heart.

Potential mentors await your discovery. Look around you and see if there is perhaps a wise person in your life, someone whose example you would like to follow. If you need a listening ear or some help sorting out a problem, ask for assistance from seasoned men and women around you. Most people are pleased to share their wisdom and expertise. We can learn lessons with the help and experience of others. We do not have to walk through every heartache and difficulty by ourselves.

Do not postpone your happiness until you have changed your circumstances to match your desires. Instead, change your interaction with the present moment by using the rich, free resources already—and always—at your disposal. The more you access these resources, the more grateful you will feel and the more you will wonder how you could ever have missed out on so much.

Life favors those who open to it. Taste and experience life's gifts as often as you can and, as you do, give thanks. God appreciates our expressions of gratitude and responds by helping us expand. We find increased optimism and renewal in spirit. When our spirits are clear and our energies are flowing we open the way for miracles.

EXERCISE:

As you continue to clarify your life purpose, remember to be aware of what life is offering you right now.

1. Rate yourself. On a scale of 1 to 10, (1 is oblivious, 10 is total appreciation) how grateful are you? How aware are you of the resources listed above?

2. What challenges in your life are keeping you from seeing and enjoying life's little blessings?

3. Look at your daily schedule. How can you integrate gratitude into your routine? For example, perhaps you could remind yourself of God's gifts before you get out of bed in the morning, when you eat your mid-day meal and when you lie down to sleep.

4. Begin practicing gratitude right now. Take five minutes and write down every positive thing in your life, big and small. When you finish your list, close your eyes and say a prayer of thanks.

5. Now that you have completed this exercise, rate yourself again. After taking stock of your blessings, on a scale of 1 to 10, how grateful are you now?

Meditation: Food For Thought

"Give thanks for a little and you will find a lot."
—The Hausa of Nigeria

"The moment one gives close attention to anything,
even a blade of grass, it becomes a mysterious, awesome,
indescribably magnificent world in itself."
—Henry Miller

"There are only two ways to live your life. One is as though
nothing is a miracle. The other is as though everything
is a miracle."
—Albert Einstein

Chapter Five

Begin
to Dream Again

KEY QUESTION:
If I could experience anything in life, what would it be?

AFFIRMATION:
I allow myself to dream and imagine.

We have looked at the legacy we want to leave. We have begun to use our inner systems to get to know ourselves. We have turned what we do not like into criteria for what we do want. And, we are finding ways to accept and appreciate our current circumstances. We are building a foundation to clarify our purpose and transform our lives from the inside out.

While we are patiently dealing with our present situations personally and professionally, we can invite growing clarity by beginning to dream again.

Please remember this chapter is about dreaming, not taking radical outward action. If you are like most of my clients, you have been discovering, as you have opened to what you desire, that there is a voice inside you saying, "That idea is not going to work. . . . They will not agree with my decision. . . . What will people think? . . . It is too much of a risk. . . . That could never be possible for me. . . ." In other words, you are uncovering the invisible belief systems that have been governing your choices.

As we have grown up, we have adopted the values of our parents, our teachers and our society. Some are empowering. Others are restrictive and may no longer be working for us. I invite you to put all your fears and doubts aside.

Think about this. Life moves quickly—weeks, months and years can slip away when we move mindlessly through our daily routines. We often let the next person, activity, thought or feeling that clamors for our attention dictate how we spend our time. We also permit the voices of others, some of them no longer present in our lives, to influence or even control the decisions we make.

It is as if we are in our own boat moving down the river of life. People in other boats have thrown ropes to us to "help us" move along the river. We accepted some of these lines and as a result, we are pulled this way and that. We bump and splash erratically rather than navigating our own boat wisely through the currents.

I invite you to drop the mental ropes and get out your oars. How would you like to steer your boat? What stops do you want to make? What experiences are you longing to have on your journey down Life's river?

Begin to dream again!

Guidelines for Dreaming

As you start this creative process, follow these guidelines:

Throw out all the "rules" you have adopted from others and those you have imposed upon yourself such as, "You can't do it that way. You must follow a traditional path like everyone else.

Fit in. That's impossible. You are being impractical. Nobody's done that before, why would you think you can?"

Do not get in your own way. Determine not to listen to the voices of self-limitation and fear as they whisper to you, "This is silly. I can't change my life. I can't be, have and experience what I want." There are possibilities available to you beyond what you can conceive. Why not open to this? Do not allow yourself to shut down your dreams before you even give them a chance to bubble up. If you are going to stop yourself, at least take a good look at what your heart wants to envision before you close it down. That way you will have a sense of what you've decided to relinquish.

Set aside preconceived notions about who you are. Who you were yesterday does not predict who you are today—unless, of course, you believe it does. Each of us is free to reinvent and reconfigure ourselves as often as we would like. People may have told you that you need to follow a certain path or that you are not gifted enough to succeed in other fields. Believe in yourself rather than the opinions of others. You can try anything. Explore "you." Stretch. Find out what you like, where your aptitudes are, what sparks your curiosity and what you would find exhilarating. Experiment. Have fun imagining.

Listen to your own voice. While your dreams are young and growing inside you, choose wisely who you share them with. Do not cast your dreams before swine. Other people may have plenty of advice to offer. People caught in negativity and judgment are all too willing to tell you what you should do from their perspective.

If you get stuck, just take a break. At first, it may feel uncomfortable to let yourself explore what you really want. That is okay. New processes feel challenging when we begin them. Soon, you will get the hang of dreaming big and following the voice of your heart.

If a thought like, "I don't know how to find my dreams," comes to mind, replace it with a prayer. Then tell yourself, "I can ask the questions in my heart. I can listen for whispers of guidance from God. My answers will emerge with some soul searching and thought."

Do not shut a dream down because you do not know HOW it can become a reality. For now, just dream. Just imagine. Just get a clearer picture of what you really want. Ask God for direction.

When we hold a question in our heart, we are bound to find the answer. Open your eyes and ears. You never know when just the right someone or something will show up to give you the key idea, item or opportunity you need to bring your dream into focus and eventually to manifest your dream.

These no-rule, no-limit guidelines are just to say, let go of all the "Shoulds," "Musts" and "Have-to's." Be completely free as you dream.

EXERCISE:

It's time to play!

This exercise will help you become even clearer about the fulfilling experiences you want to welcome into your life. Be lighthearted as you answer these questions. In fact, let the voice of your Inner Child guide you to a deeper understanding of your desires.

1. Rediscover what brings you joy. Think back to who you were at ages 5, 10 and 15. (If you cannot remember, ask your parents or others who knew you at those points in your life.) Answer these questions to trigger memories of your personal passions and aptitudes.

    a. What were your favorite subjects in school?
    b. What activities couldn't you get enough of?
    c. What made your heart beat faster?
    d. What dominated your thinking?

2. Using any insights you have gained, answer the following question, "If I could do ANYTHING, absolutely ANYTHING, I wanted to do in each area of my life, what would it be?"

    Pour your answers out on paper. Start with words. Unleash your creativity. Engage all your senses. Think in bright colors. You can even use crayons, colored pencils and paints. Draw pictures or symbols of your desires. Try to see, hear, taste, smell and touch your dream. Let your body experience the emotions that would come from living your dreams.

3. Create a Dream Box. This can be any container large enough to hold small pictures, clippings and tiny objects. You might want to make it special by decorating it and naming it. Page through a few magazines or newspapers. Pay attention to words, pictures and symbols that generate enthusiasm and excitement in you. Cut out these images and words. Put them in your Dream Box. Continue this process over a period of several weeks or months.

4. Create a Dream Board. Look at the words and images in your Dream Box. Spread them out on the floor or table in front of you. Take a piece of paper, poster board or cardboard and use glue or tape to make a collage that incorporates the words and pictures that represent your dreams.

5. Place your Dream Board in a place where you can see it every day. Take time to really look at it. By doing these exercises you are planting seeds. By reminding yourself of your dreams every day, you are watering the seeds. Every day affirm, "These dreams are living threads in the reality unfolding in my life every day. I invite these dreams to manifest in the best possible way."

Meditation: Food For Thought

"Cut not the wings of your dreams, for they are the heartbeat
and the freedom of your soul."
—Flavia

"Every great dream begins with a dreamer. Always remember,
you have within you the strength, the patience, and the
passion to reach for the stars to change the world."
—Harriet Tubman

Chapter Six

Write Your Next Chapter

KEY QUESTION:
What will I pen in my next chapter?

AFFIRMATION:
I set a clear intention for my next chapter of life.

Many of my life coaching clients find it helpful to view their lives as a book with many chapters. Some chapters might represent years; others might be shorter, covering only three to six-month periods. During weekly sessions with my clients, I help them write (or sketch, if they prefer art) a detailed description of who they want to be, what they want to do and how they would like to feel in the next stage of their journey.

By creating a Dream Box or a Dream Board you have taken some snapshots of what you desire. Now let's use them to construct your next chapter. This is an exercise to help you clarify your next steps, goals you would like to work toward, people you want to meet and adventures you would like to have in a relative time-frame. The point is not to generate fixed expectations, but rather to create conscious possible scenarios that you would welcome and enjoy. It is good to dream and plan. But be aware: when you become active in co-creating your journey, life has a way of bringing you joyful surprises that far exceed your original ideas.

EXERCISE:

Imagine today that you are the author of the book of your life. You are also the main character. It is up to you to develop the roles that you play in the story. It is also your responsibility to guide the storyline. What would you like to see happen in your next chapter?

Honor this process by setting aside 30 minutes to an hour to get started. Once you begin you will find that your ideas will grow and you will have more to add to your chapter over upcoming weeks and months.

Get into a relaxed frame of mind. Try to eliminate all other distractions. Play some inspiring music. Allow yourself to feel exhilarated and hopeful as you embark on this creative adventure. As you work, be happy. Have fun.

1. Gather all the insights you have gleaned from this book so far: review your journal, refer to your list of negatives transformed into positives and utilize your Dream Box and/or Board.

2. Quiet yourself and invite Divine guidance. Picture what makes your heart sing. Ask God for clarity as you contemplate the questions in this exercise. Let the answers come from the deepest part of your heart and spirit rather than from your mind alone.

3. Consider the time frame for your next chapter: Will it be three months, six months, one year or maybe three to five years?

4. On a blank piece of paper in your journal, playfully begin to draft your next chapter. Describe your character.

    a. What qualities will your character exhibit through the next chapter? For example, energy, determination, courage, patience, resilience. Make your own list.

    b. What life and professional skills will you develop?

    c. What roles do you see yourself playing? For example, spouse, manager, employer/employee, networker, leader/follower, hero/instigator.

5. Use the questions on the following pages to stimulate your thinking for each area of your life. Read through all the questions, then choose a few that resonate with you. Make notes as you go. Let them guide you and support you as you imagine your next chapter.

6. Each day this week choose one category of questions and answer them in as much detail as you can.

7. Keep in mind that there will be many chapters ahead. Narrow your focus and choose a few key desires/goals as priorities for this chapter.

8. Create a title for your next chapter. For example, "New Horizons," "Venturing into New Territory," "Quickly Progressing," "Finding New Love," "Adventure of a Lifetime," "Soaring Higher," "The Big Win," "Taking a Leap of Faith," "Making a Difference," or "Loving deeply."

You have planted seeds for your next chapter in your heart and mind. Allow them to incubate. Take a break from thinking about them intentionally. See what additional ideas naturally pop into your mind. Record your inspirations in your journal.

You have engaged in writing one chapter. Consider using this exercise periodically. Many of my clients revisit this exercise every three to four months.

Keep in mind that consciously or unconsciously you are authoring the book of your life.

Questions for Developing Your Next Chapter

Career / Life Work

How can you maximize your learning in your current job?

How can you bring positive energy and enthusiasm to the projects you are working on?

What new tasks and projects would you like to participate in?

Is growing in your current job part of your next chapter or do you envision making a change?

How do you see your on-the-job relationships improving: with co-workers, with management, with customers/clients?

How can you build your professional skills or qualifications?

Can you see yourself with a career mentor? Who comes to mind?

Will you be mentoring someone? Who comes to mind?

How many hours a day will you work?

How many days a week will you work?

Will you build flexibility into your schedule?

Will you take work home with you? If so, how will you integrate it with your family time?

Finances

Is your bank account balance growing?

Are current debts being resolved?

Do you envision new sources of income? What are they?

Can you see money flowing to you easily, arriving in unexpected or miraculous ways?

How will you use discretionary funds?

How will you share your resources with others?

Relationships

Are toxic relationships moving toward healing or beginning to dissolve?

In what wholesome ways are your friendships improving?

Are new friends appearing? What are these new friends like? Do they share interests that support your personal growth and life purpose?

What social events and activities are you enjoying with friends?

Can you envision any long-term conflict with a friend or family member reaching a peaceful conclusion?

Are family relationships becoming more respectful, mutually supportive and joyful?

What positive changes are occurring with your significant other?

If you do not have a significant other, what kind of person do you see yourself getting to know? (List detailed traits you desire.)

What characteristics define the new relationship?

Health

How would you like to feel when you wake up each day? How do you intend to care for your body?

How will you keep your body physically fit?

What eating habits will you choose to foster good health?

How will you resolve any current or new health issues?

How will you move toward increasing acceptance of your body?

Emotional Health

Are you listening to the guidance your emotions offer?

Are you seeking help in understanding deep emotional struggles?

Are you able to freely and appropriately express your emotions?

Spiritual

What steps are you taking to open your spirit to Divine truth?

Are you beginning and ending your day with prayer and gratitude?

Are you spending time in meditation and/or reading from a sacred text?

Are you participating in a community of like-minded individuals who support the growth of your faith?

Are you tuning in to God's guidance?

Are you clarifying your truth?

How are you integrating your truth into your daily routines?

Service

How do you see yourself showing kindness and compassion as you move through your day?

How are you using your passions and skills to make a difference in your community?

How are you becoming the change you want to see in the world?

Recreation, Personal Adventure and Self-Development

What do you see yourself doing for the sheer fun of it?

Will you be traveling to new places?

What might you dare to do that you never before thought feasible?

What funny, thought provoking, or uplifting television shows and movies are you watching?

What books are you reading for pleasure?

What materials are you using for self-development? Audio, visual, in-person workshops and seminars, web-based learning, etc.?

Meditation: Food For Thought

"Wake up each day
knowing the page is blank.
Imagine your story unfolding.
See it in vivid detail.
You will be surprised, amazed—

Write your story as you consciously intend it.
Write your story just as you want it to be.

The moments you take to determine your story
are worth the effort.

What you write, will open the possibilities for what you live."

—Patricia Omoqui, The Thought Dr.™

"You will become as small as your controlling desire; as great as your dominant aspiration."
—James Allen

"If one advances confidently in the direction of his dreams, and endeavors to live the life which he has imagined, he will meet with a success unexpected in common hours."
—Henry David Thoreau

Chapter Seven

Open to Your Answers and Follow Through

KEY QUESTION:
How will I know my next step?

AFFIRMATION:
I trust that I am always guided to the next step to take
in fulfilling my purpose.

Now that you have written your next chapter, you are no doubt asking yourself, "What do I do now?" You are eager to translate your inner desires into daily realities. When a person asks the right questions, answers begin to appear. You begin to notice ideas all around you. You find articles and books. You experience "aha" moments. As you talk about your dreams, friends, family members and mentors may offer their advice. Now with all this varied input to consider, you are probably still confused about how to determine the right next step to take.

Recently I had an email exchange with a client whose dream is financial freedom. He was frustrated. Someone had borrowed money but had not paid it back. He sought advice and received a variety of conflicting suggestions. Now he was asking me what he should do. I suggested that he take time to quiet his mind and ask to be guided to the next step. His reaction was, "Is that all you are going to tell me?"

People often do not like suggestions I offer because they want me or another "outside authority" to answer their problem with the exact step they should take or the precise way to move forward.

While we can offer ideas and brainstorm solutions with others, we cannot solve anyone else's problems.

My job as a life coach is not to tell you what to do. Rather, it is to help you realize that you have guidance within yourself to navigate life's journey. Each of us must listen to our guidance and follow through. My goal is to empower you, not to make you dependent on me.

People find their own answers when they take time to do so. Think of times when you have asked for advice. Perhaps, someone gave you just the right solution. How did you know? You knew it was right when you pulled it inside yourself and realized it felt right to you. On the other hand, how many times have you experienced immediate inner resistance to suggestions? You somehow understood this advice would not work for you.

Nobody knows your situation better than you. If you are going to clarify your purpose and live your dreams, you must consciously tune in to your inner guidance.

We humans like shortcuts. We think that getting advice is easier than taking time to listen to the voice of God within. You have internal expertise. You have built-in systems, or mechanisms, for connecting to Divine wisdom. (See Chapter Two.) People who insist on giving you "the answer" are unknowingly asking you to bypass the confidence that develops when you follow your inner knowing.

The step for the next moment is always there for us, but we ignore it because we do not trust ourselves. Then we move through the situation with a victim mentality; we plead with those around us, "Please help me! What should I do?" Each of us has access to the inspired thought, word or action called for in each moment. Insights pour to us and through us, but we often do not recognize them or we hear them and brush them off. Are you listening to your intuition? Are you noticing that occasionally the perfect response to a situation pops into your mind? Are you acting on inner instructions that come to you repeatedly? Do you follow through on your inner guidance?

A few months ago, a client told me that when he was getting ready for work, he received a flood of amazing ideas for steps he could take during the day to help him in his business. Unfortunately, he would get busy and forget the inspirations he had been given. We agreed that he should take a moment to jot down his inspirations. By carrying a small notepad and pen he was able to capture his insights. He experienced fantastic results as he implemented these solutions.

If you are ready to tap into your inner guidance as you move forward to make your next chapter a reality, here are some suggestions that help me and others I work with.

Clarify your questions. When I ask my clients, "What do you need to know now?" they often say, "I'm not sure." Take time to get specific on what questions need to be answered next. Write them down. Then, ask for guidance. Once you ask the question, let it go. Do not try to figure out the answer with your thinking mind. Turn your attention to something else and trust that the answer will come at the perfect moment. Expect it and be prepared to act on it.

Slow down. Find time to quiet your mind. We know the value of stepping back to quiet ourselves, but we feel caught in an endless cycle of activity. Our minds and our bodies are in constant motion—or commotion. I encourage you to find at least 30 seconds to a minute several times a day to turn off your mind and listen for inner guidance. Carve out a specific time in your schedule every day for five minutes of mental rest. (If you can do more, then try 10 or 15 minutes.) The more you listen for guidance, the more you will hear it.

Do not limit the ways you can receive guidance. The door to Divine guidance is open to all. It can come through a song on the radio. Or perhaps you are drawn to a particular book. A co-worker may make a casual remark that will strike you deep within. A billboard might provide the perfect message of encouragement. God is not limited in the means he can use. Be aware. Enjoy the humor and creativity with which the guidance appears.

Write your guidance down. You never know when you may receive inspiration. Carry a small notebook and a pen. If you record your ideas, you will find yourself with a roadmap to your dreams.

Let peace lead you. As you listen, ideas will flow. If you receive a variety of ideas and you are not sure which ones to use, ask yourself, "Which of these ideas give me peace?" Do not move forward while you are in conflict. Wait. Weigh each option in your heart. Your intellect and fears can generate discord and confusion. God directs us through peace.

Take consistent, daily baby steps. If you are going to live your life purpose, it is time to start now. Take simple steps each day. For instance, while I was in my corporate job I knew I wanted to become a life coach. So every day, I made time to move in the direction of my dreams. I sat in silence. I wrote in my journal. I read books. I participated in weekend and other extended trainings. I shared what I was learning. Soon people were coming to me with questions. I began coaching for free in order to practice. I made business cards. Eventually, I got my first client and built an evening practice. You get the idea. I wear a necklace that reminds me, "The journey of a thousand miles starts with the first step." I encourage you to take your first step. Begin to taste the joy of progress.

Leave the results to God. We get frustrated when our seeds do not bear fruit as early as we think they should. Do not lose heart. Be patient. Find happiness in simple things. Each part of your journey teaches you a lesson. Do your part: ask the questions, listen for the answers and take daily action. In time, breakthroughs come and your work will culminate in joyful achievement and satisfaction.

EXERCISE:

Add this process to your daily routine. Give it a try right now.

1. Review your next chapter. Write down one or two pressing questions for which you need answers to begin moving forward.

2. Say a prayer, "Please guide me to my next steps and any insights I need."

3. Slow your mind and breathe deeply for a few moments.

4. Write down any answers that come to mind.

5. If answers do not come right away, affirm: I am grateful that my answers come to me in perfect timing and in miraculous ways.

6. Walk through your day expecting to receive insights. Keep a pen and journal handy so that when your ideas come, you can write them down.

7. Take daily baby steps toward manifesting your next chapter. Be committed. Follow through on each insight you receive.

Meditation: Food For Thought

"We don't need someone to show us the ropes. We are the
ones we've been waiting for. Deep inside us we know the
feelings we need to guide us. Our task is to learn to trust our
inner knowing."
—Sonia Johnson

"No man is great enough or wise enough for any of us to sur-
render our destiny to. The only way in which anyone can lead
us is to restore to us the belief in our own guidance."
—Henry Miller

"Goals are dreams we convert to plans and take
action to fulfill."
—Zig Ziglar

Chapter Eight

Face Your Fears

KEY QUESTION:
What fears are hindering me?

AFFIRMATION:
I examine my fears, learn from them and move beyond them.

Now you have a dream in your heart. You are getting a clearer vision of what you want to experience in the next chapter of your life. So, beware! You will no doubt begin to hear the voices of the "Fear Monsters." Fear Monsters come in all shapes and sizes. They lurk in the darkness of our subconscious just beyond the periphery of our attention. They flood our thought streams with insidious questions about our worth, our abilities and our resources. Their goal is to sabotage us, to keep us stuck. Nothing pleases a Fear Monster more than clouding your mind with confusion and poisoning your heart with doubt.

You panic. You hear yourself thinking, "Am I crazy to believe that I could live my dream? I will fail. I will embarrass myself. I will never be able to make this dream a reality." Paralysis sets in quickly when we allow the Fear Monsters free rein. At this point, our thoughts tell us to rush back to the apparent safety of the status quo. What we fail to realize is that running from Fear Monsters is exactly what they want. When we attempt to "escape," the shadows of these fears seem to tower over us from behind. Our perceptions become distorted. Our thoughts conjure horrific pictures of possible disaster. We imagine the fear to be far more imposing, dangerous and powerful than it actually is. This is what American

President Franklin Delano Roosevelt was referring to when he said, "The only thing we have to fear is fear itself."

Why not try a new approach? Rather than hiding from your fear, pull out a flashlight and a magnifying glass. Draw the fear into the center of your awareness. Get as close to it as you can. Experience the fear. Examine it. Get to know it with the same intimacy as you are getting to know your dreams.

Get To Know Your Fear Monsters

What are these Fear Monsters anyway? Are they real entities out to ruin us? No. They are merely mental constructions, emotionally charged negative beliefs, that we have been conditioned to accept as true. They project dreadful, unavoidable outcomes to which we bow. We believe them to be pointless to question and impossible to overcome. If we continue to cower to fear, it becomes overwhelming. It is not fear itself, but our belief in fear that creates misery, depression and immobility.

Our fears typically come from unquestioned beliefs about how life works. Until we face these beliefs, they linger deep in our subconscious and we remain unaware of the impact they have on us every day. The following are common fearful beliefs that influence us: I am unworthy, inadequate and undeserving; I cannot trust Life; I am not safe and supported; Things do not work out for my best; As hard as the present challenges are, the future will be worse. Do these thoughts sound familiar to you? These invisible, underlying beliefs hinder you. Unless you question them, they will keep you from living a rich and fulfilling life.

The Fear Cycle

Let us look at how fear works.

First, a limiting belief surfaces. You think, "I can't do this." When you give that thought attention, it generates a corresponding emotion. You feel disappointed and sad. The emotions flow into your body. Your energy drains away. Your stomach is in knots. Then, based on how you feel physically, you act or you take no action at all. You slump into your chair with a sigh. You let your dreams die.

Allow me to illustrate this from my personal experience. I grew up in a family that believed money was scarce. We were taught to economize continually. Money was for necessities not for enjoyment. Money issues caused disagreements and distress. As a child, I adopted fearful beliefs without even knowing it: Money is hard to come by. I had better hold on to what I get. Spending for personal enjoyment is wasteful. Don't take financial risks. Ultimately, thoughts of money brought up fear and inner conflict.

Fast forward to my adult years. I had a job with a great salary. I outgrew the challenges it offered. I dreamed of a new vocation as a life coach, speaker and writer. Yet, whenever I considered making a career change, I found myself incapacitated with fear. My body became tense. My stomach churned. My heart pounded. My thoughts attacked me, "I must be insane. Giving up a stable income would be irresponsible. How will I meet my bills if I go out on a limb and try something new?" Again and again, I listened to the fear and stayed where I was. I suppressed my dreams even though my heart yearned to pursue them.

As I quieted myself and observed my fears, I began to understand the cycle: a thought surfaces; I focus on it; I feel an emotion; the emotion affects my body; the effect on my body influences my behavior. I did not want to live like a poor bird caged by my fear. I decided to welcome my Fear Monsters, one at a time, into my awareness and study them. I asked God for help.

Invite Your Fears to a Meeting

I invited my fears to regular meetings. They came hoping to intimidate me. As I met with each one, I allowed myself to feel it.

I realized that consciously experiencing the fear would not hurt me. I discovered the fears had, in fact, been crying for my attention. By dialoguing with my fears, I tamed them and was able to see them in a new light. As their energy transformed, I noticed they were actually bringing me gifts. Each fear offered me an opportunity to resolve pain and confusion, and end self-doubt.

I asked myself, "Could I believe that money is abundant rather than scarce? Is it possible there are other ways to define being responsible?" Perhaps it would be irresponsible for me NOT to find my purpose and fulfill it.

That is when my breakthroughs began to happen. As I confronted my fears and questioned the beliefs behind them, I realized that I could choose to view my life differently. I was relieved. When a Fear Monster spoke, I no longer ran from it or locked it in the basement. I chose not to tolerate the uneasiness and anxiety of trying to sidestep my fears. Rather, I told the fear, "I welcome you into my awareness. I am going to take a close look at you now. I am determined to see you differently. I accept the gifts you have for me."

Periodically a fear I thought I had dealt with reappears to nag me. However, when a fear tries to drag me into the past or into the future, (places of worry and doubt), I look straight at it and say, "No!" Instead, I pull myself back into the present moment and ask for Divine guidance. I choose to find a new perspective.

I no longer am willing to live like an imprisoned bird, trapped by fearful beliefs. I have taken my cage apart one fear at a time. I am transforming it into a perch from which I can fly.

I have encouraged you to dream big, to get a clear picture of what you want in each aspect of your life. It is possible to create the life of your dreams—IF you have the courage to confront your fears. It is possible if you replace draining, limiting beliefs and thoughts with positive, empowering beliefs and thoughts.

Your Fears Help You Grow

Get to know your fears. If you do, you will gradually come to see them as helpful learning partners. You are not your fear. You are much greater, much grander, than any fear you may be experiencing. You only begin to know this if you calmly question your fearful thoughts. Honor each fear as it calls for your attention by shining the light of love on it. Be patient. Be persistent. Face each doubt and worry again and again. They will shrink and dissolve as they transform into deep insights that set you free.

Your fears are offering you the opportunity to grow in consciousness, to stretch your mind and heart, to expand your perspective, to discover the depth and breadth of your true being. Confronting your fears is an essential step in clarifying and living your life purpose.

EXERCISE:

Observe your mind. List your fears in your journal. For each fear, answer these questions.

1. What is the fear telling me? Write your anxious thoughts down in detail so you can see it clearly. I strongly recommend you DO NOT skip this step. Writing down what your fears are saying is a means of capturing the fear so you can examine it. Fears are sneaky. If you do not capture the fear, your thoughts will shift and the fear will continue to elude you.

2. How is the fear affecting your life?

    a. When you focus on a fearful thought, what emotions do you feel?

    b. How do you feel physically when you buy into a negative, limiting thought?

3. What does your life look like without the fearful thinking?

    a. Without this fear, what would you be doing to pursue your dreams and goals?

    b. Without this fear, how would you act, who would you be?

    c. What possibilities would open up in your life if you chose a different perspective?

4. Now, transform your fear into an empowering statement.

Meditation: Food For Thought

"Ultimately we know deeply that the other side of
every fear is freedom."
—Marilyn Ferguson

Chapter Nine

Surrender:
Plan A or Plan U?

KEY QUESTION:
What response will I choose when things do not go as planned?

AFFIRMATION:
I do my best. I make a plan and remain flexible. Life guides me to
my next steps. I open to all possibilities.

I had committed to my life purpose. I was facing my fears as they arose. I had left my job and begun taking life coaching clients and speaking engagements. I had used my business skills to put a plan in place that I thought would work well in making this transition to my new business. However, as we all know, while we are making plans, life happens.

Our dreams do not come to fulfillment in a vacuum. I may have become a life coach but I was and am also a wife and mother. If your vision is related to a new vocation, it must manifest as a motif in the larger mosaic that includes all your roles and responsibilities.

Here is a snapshot of the how life happened in spite of my plan. It was a Thursday, a day to work toward my goals. It did not go as I had planned. I was set for a photo-shoot. I had scheduled clients and intended to take next steps on an article for my newspaper column. Instead, Maggie, my older daughter, ended up home from school. I cancelled all appointments to take care of her.

Actually, the last several months had not been what I expected. My list of goals included finished projects, new partnerships and more speaking engagements. Little of what I originally intended had come to completion. I could have felt frustrated because I had not "reached my goals."

Yet when I sat and considered what had actually taken place, I saw that, often, I have no idea what is really best for me. I had spent more time with my children than I normally was able to. I had cooked more meals than I was used to. Other supportive roles that I tended to play only occasionally, I had been performing repeatedly with new people and in new ways. I will not lie and give the impression that this did not create inner conflict. It did. Some days, rather than relaxing into the flow, I spent time wishing that I was somewhere else doing something totally different.

Resisting what life brings creates intense stress.

Life Gives Us Opportunities to Learn

I know better. I teach the importance of living in the "Now," and I have spent several years practicing it earnestly. I understand the comfort and enjoyment found in fully embracing life moment by moment. However, it seems that God wanted me to take my practicing of presence to an even more comprehensive level: "Patricia, you say you want to become a master at staying present. Get ready, Life is about to provide you with some surprising twists and turns. Will you trust these new directions and flow calmly with the rushing river of Life or will you fight against the currents stubbornly using your energy to swim upstream to the destination you fixed in your mind?"

I admit that I often find myself turning upstream. However, my self-awareness skills are developed enough to help me tune in when my stress levels are rising and I am feeling on edge with people around me. I have to stop myself repeatedly from holding onto my "Plan A." Plan A is MY PLAN. It exists in my head. It is what my logical mind has conjured up. It is what I think I should be, do and achieve over a period of time. I am not sure why I continue to be taken by surprise when Plan A does not happen as I think it ought to. It rarely does. Inevitably, Life seems to have something else in mind, a "Plan U," Plan Universe; that is, *what the Universe under God's direction has planned for You.*

When the infinite wisdom of God serves me up the perfect dish to try, filled with unexpected ingredients and plenty of nutritional value for my ever-evolving soul, why do I get so frustrated? Things I could never have anticipated in my life occur all the time. I am both pleasantly surprised by opportunities that literally fall from heaven with no effort on my part and shocked by startling challenges in my work and relationships. One thing is certain: I am given the next set of growth opportunities perfect for my journey. And so are you.

Every Moment We Have a Choice

Oppose life or open to it? Resist this moment or surrender with a willing heart? This is our one choice every day, every hour, every minute, even every second. When we judge life to be going wrong, we feel anger, resentment, even despair. We think, "This should not be happening. It is not fair that it turned out this way. Why are things always so hard for me?" We feel victimized by the circumstances we encounter. These responses are formed based upon a belief many of us unconsciously espouse: things can go wrong in my life. Is it possible we bought into a viewpoint that is inaccurate? Perhaps the reality of the Universe is quite the reverse: each thing that occurs in my life is exactly what I need for my development.

When we assume that each moment unfolds with uncanny precision, we have new responses. "This is interesting. I did not expect this. Since this is happening, there must be something for me to learn. I release myself to the flow of Life and gracefully move with whatever this moment brings me."

A different set of questions emerges from the belief that everything happens for a reason. Rather than asking, "Why did this happen to me?" We instead ask, "How is this situation perfect for me right now? What insight can I glean about myself, my relationships and my beliefs from this seeming challenge?"

Take this apparently insignificant example of a young man about to leave for vacation. His dream was to spend time at an ocean resort. Now it was becoming a reality. He loved music and anticipated that his most precious possession, his IPod, would be his travel companion. When he boarded the flight, he realized he had dropped his IPod in the taxi. It was gone. He was angry with himself, saddened by his loss. However, since it was his practice to look for the silver lining in every situation, he curbed his stressful, negative thoughts with a question, "Is there anything good that I can find in this situation?" For awhile, resurging disappointment was so strong that not one answer came to mind, but the question itself brought a measure of relief. It helped him calm himself and reinforced his determination to have a good time.

At the end of his trip, he revisited the question. His mind flooded with insight. Without earplugs to isolate him, he had met several fascinating fellow travelers. One had suggested a restaurant with excellent food and reasonable prices. Another had mentioned a company that was hiring for just the position he was seeking (his dream job!). He had taken the time to read an uplifting book. He had tuned into the music of the children giggling as they played games in the row in front of him. He realized that his IPod was only one of many ways he could find companionship while traveling. He understood that, as always, God had his best interest in mind. Things DO happen for a reason. He was being guided.

Ask yourself, "Am I creating extra anxiety in my life because I am narrow-mindedly set on achieving Plan A? Or, am I able to step back when things appear to go wrong and watch for the emergence of Plan U?"

Caution: Resist the temptation to make your Plan A a "set-in-stone" agenda. Open to the miraculous unfolding of Plan U.

EXERCISE:

Think of something in your life right now that is not going as you planned. Write down the details and answer the following questions:

1. How is this situation perfect for me right now?

2. What insight can I glean about myself?

3. Is there anything good that I can find in this situation?

4. In what ways is this situation causing me to learn and grow as an individual, in my relationships and in the ways I handle life?

Sit quietly for a few moments. Let yourself feel the difference between your original reaction and the new responses you generated by answering these questions. Begin to notice whether you believe that something "went wrong" or whether you can see that Life is supporting you with a wiser, underlying design.

Consider repeating this exercise with other unexpected challenges you are facing. If you found this exercise helpful, write the questions down and post them somewhere you will see them often.

Meditation: Food For Thought

"Life's challenges are not supposed to paralyze you. They're
supposed to help you discover who you are."
—Bernice Johnson Reagon

"There are no failures—just experiences and your
reactions to them."
—Tom Krause

"My imperfections and failures are as much a blessing
from God as my successes and my talents and I lay them both
at his feet."
—Mahatma Gandhi

Chapter Ten

Use Your Dreams to Change the World

KEY QUESTION:
How can I use my dreams to help others?

AFFIRMATION:
I use my dreams to change the world.

Let us consider our dreams and how they relate to the dreams of others. Pull one of your dreams into your mind; for instance, becoming a successful artist or starting your own business. Do you feel as if you need to protect your idea? Is your dream a carefully guarded secret?

We may feel sometimes as if we live in a dangerous competition. We take a defensive posture as we seek to make progress toward our own goals. Unconsciously, we may believe there is a scarcity of money, time and opportunities. Therefore, we must protect ourselves from those around us if we are to succeed.

Of course, we need to be wise about maintaining our intellectual capital. However, it is possible to approach progress with a cooperative spirit rather than a competitive one.

It is important to remember that we are each a specific expression of Life, infused with the energy of our loving Creator. This pulsating Life in every one of us is eternal. Each human being is unique and has a gift to offer to the whole. Your wellbeing is vital to the wellbeing of every living thing on the planet.

Consider your body as a metaphor. If your heart is functioning at optimum levels, the other organs do not say, "Hey, why is the heart doing so well?" No. The other organs are thankful that the heart is healthy. Their ability to thrive is dependent on how well the heart functions. Conversely, the heart's fitness relies on the wellness of the lungs, the brain, the intestines—all the other organs.

When you are born, your heart does not say, "I want to do better than any other organ in this body. I'm going to prove to the body that I am the most important." It does not need to rise above the other organs and flaunt its power. It is simply the heart, with the capacity to do its best if the body as a whole is going to be nurtured.

In the same way, each of us is a member of a grand body called the human race. We cannot afford to manipulate, avoid, out do, push others away or keep them down. We need each other. Your role may be different from mine, but we each have a contribution to make.

You Influence the World

Let us come back now to the vision of what you want to create in your life. Making your dream come true does not have to reduce others' opportunities or deprive them of resources they need to fulfill their goals. The more we humans cooperate, the more we will see that there is enough for each person to have a comfortable life if all of us begin to tie our personal dreams to our vision of the world we desire to create.

When you connect your dream to your vision for the wellbeing of your community and country, you begin to see how remarkable it is to be part of the bigger picture. You see that you influence the world. You are doing this already whether you realize it or not. When you walk through a day fearful and defensive, you have a negative impact on others and your environment. When you relax and cooperate, others notice and benefit. In either case, you touch others. You influence the lives of those around you. Do not underestimate the power for good that moves into the world when your actions emerge from the energy of kindness and love.

When we become more conscious of this interconnection, we realize that we can see our dreams as ways to help bring about positive change not only for ourselves, but for our families, our communities and our nations. Accepting this reality will ignite a greater desire in your heart. You will understand that as you generate success, that success overflows into your world.

How Many People Might Benefit From Your Dream?

Go back to that dream you were picturing. Let us say you want to start a business making scarves. You have the ability to picture beautiful scarves and design them in your mind to complement the outfits of people you see walking in the street. You love lush fabrics and bold patterns. You envision them in bright colors and fascinating designs. As you are incubating your dream, do not concentrate your thoughts on how to protect your ideas or think of ways to manipulate others to make progress. Instead, consciously choose to focus your thoughts in an uplifting direction. Ask yourself, "How many people might benefit if I take action on my idea?" Then, grow your dream this way and notice the inner energy you experience.

Let us continue with the scarf maker. Of course, she wants to make money. But there is an even deeper desire driving her dream: She wants to give other people the gift of looking their best and feeling great about what they are wearing. By acknowledging this, when she receives the money from a customer, she feels the joy of mutual gain.

With these thoughts in mind, let us follow this woman as she starts her business. To get launched she will need cloth, thread, a sewing machine, sequins and beads. Picture all the merchants (and their employees) who will benefit as she buys materials and sets up her work area. Use your imagination to follow the trail of her investment money even to the point of seeing the employees of the cloth merchant taking their wages home to buy food for their families.

Now see the woman with her first batch of finished products. The scarf maker begins to barter her scarves with other vendors in the market place to get the things she needs for her family. She receives fresh produce in exchange for a scarf that the vegetable merchant will give to his wife for a special surprise. People can see the quality of love and passion in her work. Shop owners request inventory for their stores. People "ooh" and "aah" over the exquisite artistry displayed in each scarf. She is ecstatic at the response to her creation. People come to buy beautiful gifts at each shop and the shops thrive. Customers buy the scarves as gifts for others. In fact, a daughter gives one to her mom for her birthday and it creates a special bond between them.

The scarf maker's business grows. There is such demand for her products that she hires several seamstresses. Now they benefit. They have the money they need to send their children to school. As her business bank account balance increases, the scarf maker is able to help family members and relatives with their daily needs. In fact, with her growing financial success, she is even able to lend money to a family member who is ready to launch a small business of his own.

One person's dream is helping other people have a better quality of life.

Your Dreams Can Create a Legacy of Love

Our dreams are connected to the whole. As one person does well, the others can flourish. When we incubate a dream, we can keep in mind not just our own success but the success of others. In doing so, we add another whole dimension of understanding and joyful energy to pursuing and realizing our goal.

This can be done with any dream you have, even a desire for a loving relationship. You can take a relationship and find ways that it can create a nourishing-flourishing effect that ripples to the people around you.

Remember what you give is what you receive. As Sir James Barrie said, "Those who bring sunshine into the lives of others cannot keep it from themselves." If you paint a dream with colors of kindness, helpfulness and prosperity, you will bring kindness, helpfulness and prosperity to yourself.

Wouldn't it feel even richer if while creating your own personal wealth and success, you also created a legacy of love, making the world better as you did?

EXERCISE:

Choose one of your personal dreams and connect it to your vision for a better world.

1. Write a description of your dream. Referencing the scarf-maker example above, close your eyes and let your own dream grow in your imagination.

2. List steps you will take to make your dream a reality. Look at the steps one at a time and ask, "How might others benefit as I take action on my idea?" Explore every angle you can trying to envision the ways that your ideas will touch the lives of others in a positive way.

3. Consider using this simple prayer or compose your own.

    "Dear God, as I take steps to live my purpose, help me to act from the energy of kindness and love. Please use my success to multiply the success of others. Give me the vision to see how my dreams are helping me create a legacy of love. May all of us learn to work together to create a world in which all beings thrive."

Meditation: Food For Thought

"People have been known to achieve more as a result
of working with others than against them."
—Dr. Allan Fromme

"It is literally true that you can succeed best and quickest by
helping others to succeed."
—Napoleon Hill

Seven Powerful Keys to Success

I congratulate you on consciously choosing this journey of growth and challenge. This will lead you to a life rich in meaning and purpose. Keep going! As you continue on this path, here are some vital points to keep in mind.

Key 1:
Your dreams are YOURS.

Only you can determine what makes your heart sing. No one can pursue your dreams for you. No one can force you to do this. The vision and the motivation must come from inside you. It must sustain you on your journey. When things seem tense and the outlook appears bleak, only you can know that you are exactly where you need to be to remain true to yourself.

Key 2:
Create a supportive team.

Surround yourself with friends and family members you can trust. In dark moments when you are unable to hear your heart's song, you want people around you who can sing it back to you. Adventurers can benefit from having as a sounding board, those who understands the challenges they are facing. Seek as a mentor, someone who can offer 20/20 hindsight to provide you with needed foresight.

Key 3:
Do not be surprised to encounter naysayers.

Do not be caught off guard when someone questions your dreams or scoffs at your goals. Accept this. It is part of the journey. It is up to you to believe in the value and beauty of your own dreams. When you are faced by a naysayer, do not interpret their comments as a personal affront. Instead, take what they offer under advisement. When you are alone, ask yourself, "What helpful insights can I gain from that interaction?" Then listen to your inner guidance and follow your heart. This is your life, not theirs. To maintain your balance, spend time with people who are also focused on fulfilling their life purpose.

Key 4:
Be humble and honest.

The path to your dream may not always seem clear. You will no doubt experience times of uncertainty. It is okay if you do not know the next step or the solution to the current problem. Let go of your pride and be willing to be in the unknown. Relax your mind and open to hearing the answers you need.

Key 5:
Challenges will mature you and help your dreams to evolve.

Almost always manifesting a dream into reality is a slow process. Often it feels as if you take a step forward only to be set a half-step back. You think you have found the perfect opportunity. Then you discover crucial information: somehow this "golden opportunity" is not for you. It is natural to feel disappointment; however, choose not to wallow in frustration. Life inevitably takes surprising twists and turns. Choose to believe that everything happens for a reason. Calm down. Ask for clarity. Use the insights you gain from each experience to adapt and grow your dreams. As Martin Luther King, Jr. once said, "The true measure of a man is not how he behaves in moments of comfort and convenience but how he stands at times of controversy and challenge." When life seems most difficult, it is actually offering you the chance to draw on the deep power that exists inside you.

Key 6:
Find a positive way to deal with "failure."

Every new situation you encounter, every new skill you try—no matter the outcome—results in growth. "Failures" are opportunities to gain understanding and wisdom for your next attempt at success. That is what Thomas Edison thought. When criticized for his many failures to make the first incandescent light bulb, he responded, "I have not failed. I have just found ten thousand ways that do not work." Always remember, your personal value lies in who you are not in the results of your actions. The pressures you face as you move toward your goals will force you to align inside. One day you will realize that you have become a living diamond.

Key 7:
Living your life purpose is a long-term commitment.

Following your dreams will lead to some memorable milestones and exhilarating moments of achievement. However, times like these are usually reached by those who settle in for the long haul. The daily nitty-gritty work for excellence and success takes patient, day-by-day persistence. So make the best of each day. Hum a tune. Be grateful for every blessing. Look forward to breakthroughs, they are coming. In the meantime, find joy and happiness in every ordinary experience. Every smile, every word, every simple deed infused with love will deeply enrich you and those around you.

Key Questions to
Clarify Your Purpose and Live It

Why am I here? What is my purpose?

How do I want to be remembered when my journey is done?

How do I REALLY feel about my life?

How can I shift my focus from what I do not like
to what I do like?

What good is in my life already?

If I could experience anything in life, what would it be?

What will I pen in my next chapter?

How will I know my next step?

What fears are hindering me?

What response will I choose when things do not go as planned?

How can I use my dreams to help others?

Affirmations to
Clarify Your Purpose and Live It

I wake up to my life. I wake up to my power.

I open to my deeper purpose.

I tune in to the way I feel about my life and stay tuned in.

I turn negative experiences into helpful insights.

I am grateful for the good in my current circumstances.

There are blessings in every moment.

I allow myself to dream and imagine.

I set a clear intention for my next chapter of life.

I trust that I am always guided to the next step to take in
fulfilling my purpose.

I examine my fears, learn from them and move beyond them.

I do my best. I make a plan and remain flexible. Life guides me
to my next steps.

I open to all possibilities.

I use my dreams to change the world.

About The Authors

Patricia Omoqui, The Thought Dr.™

Patricia Omoqui, The Thought Dr.™, is an internationally recognized speaker, life coach and author. Patricia is a Princeton graduate, former professional basketball player and highly successful business woman and entrepreneur.

Patricia is a featured weekly columnist for Vanguard Newspaper's Allure Magazine (Nigeria) and the Daily Dispatch (Ghana). In her column, she provides insights that are helping her readers live to their full potential. Her inspirational speaking clips have aired on Silverbird TV (Nigeria), Crystal TV (Ghana) and MindTV (USA).

111

Patricia helps people wake up to their God-given power and remember they are here on earth for a very important purpose. Her energizing seminars teach practical principles that help individuals transform their lives quickly and simply. Patricia delivers keynote addresses at global events with Fortune 500 executives, government officials and community leaders in attendance.

Drawing on her experience as a business consultant, corporate manager, Six Sigma Green Belt and mediator, she provides customized business training on topics such as Leadership, Teamwork, Excellence in Work and Life, Process Improvement and Customer Service.

Patricia offers one-on-one or group coaching to business executives and established leaders who want to expand their potential to a new level of satisfaction and success.

Patricia Omoqui is an American married to a Nigerian. She is a passionate agent of change, working earnestly to positively influence the world.

To learn more about Patricia's work and to sign up for Patricia's free, daily inspirational email list, *Food For Thought*, visit her website: http://www.patriciaomoqui.com.

About The Authors

Gayle Dulcey

Gayle Dulcey is an educational and archetypal psychologist, award-winning teacher/professor, and experienced editor. She currently works as a spiritual life coach and counselor. Gayle loves learning. She holds degrees in English, English Education, Linguistics, Ethics and Spiritual Education and has completed over 100 hours of doctoral work in Educational Psychology, Archetypes, and Wisdom Studies.

Gayle's passion as an archetypal psychologist is to help people identify underlying negative patterns they repeat, find and face the roots of their fears, forgive themselves and others, and move on. As a spiritual life coach, Gayle leads groups to healing, using a system of spiritual psychotherapy that interfaces well with AA, NA and other 12-Step programs. As a counselor, she offers intensive one-on-one sessions to individuals willing to own their issues and take steps toward positive personal transformation.

Gayle is Patricia's trusted mentor, friend, and mother. Her goal is to support people in regaining their sense of wholeness and power so they can engage fully in life.

CPSIA information can be obtained at www.ICGtesting.com

261152BV00001B/4/P